AF321557

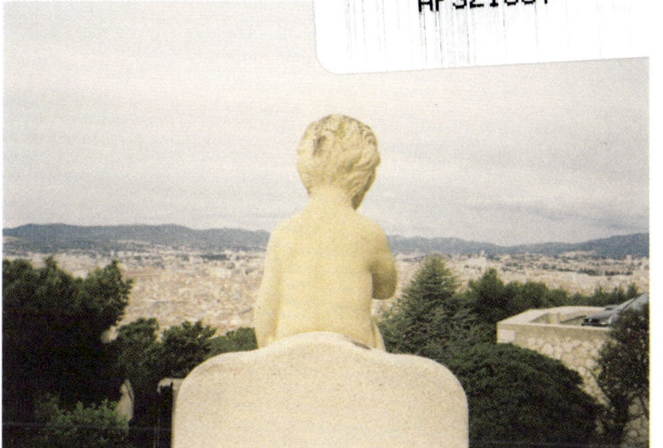

Bum Bum Tam Tam

The day has come
Like a song
On a playlist
It takes you by surprise
And feels as good as raining
Really you don't like it?
I'm assuming it never helped you fly
You never flew
Of your body while dancing?
I am constantly
Three
Stories
High

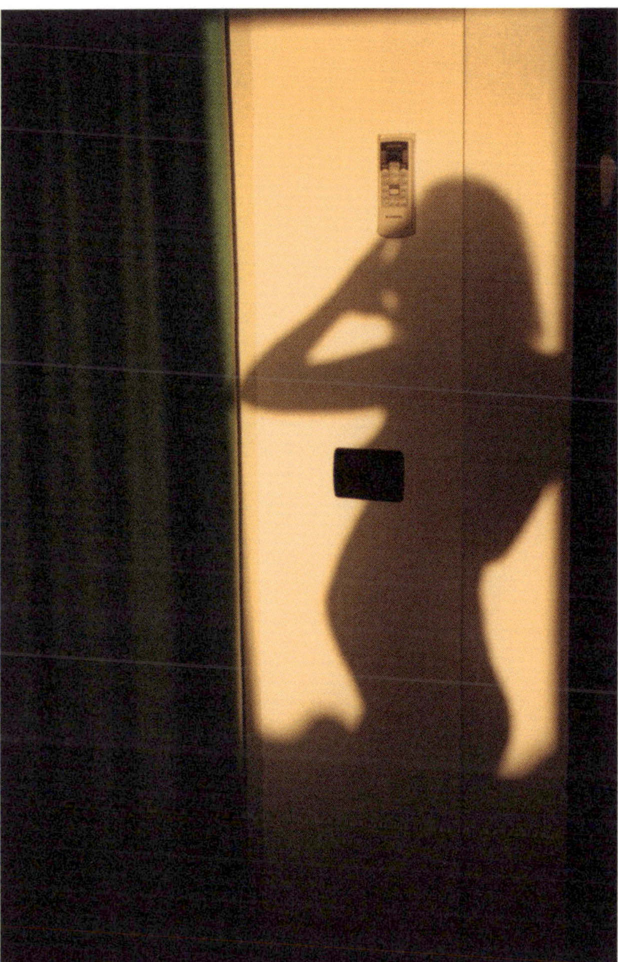

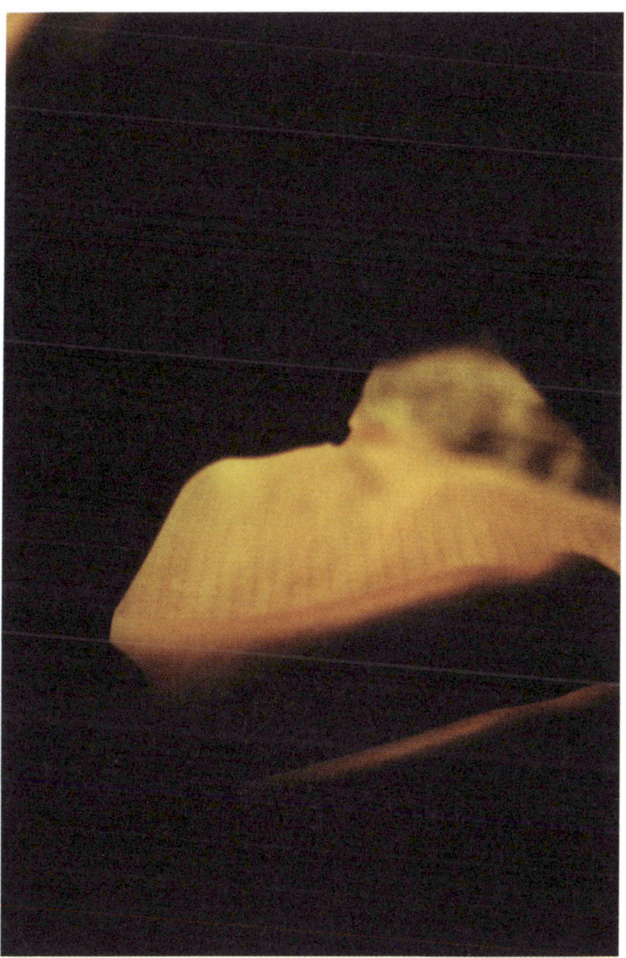

Easily

We will walk on the sea
Easily
We never learned to swim
There was no need

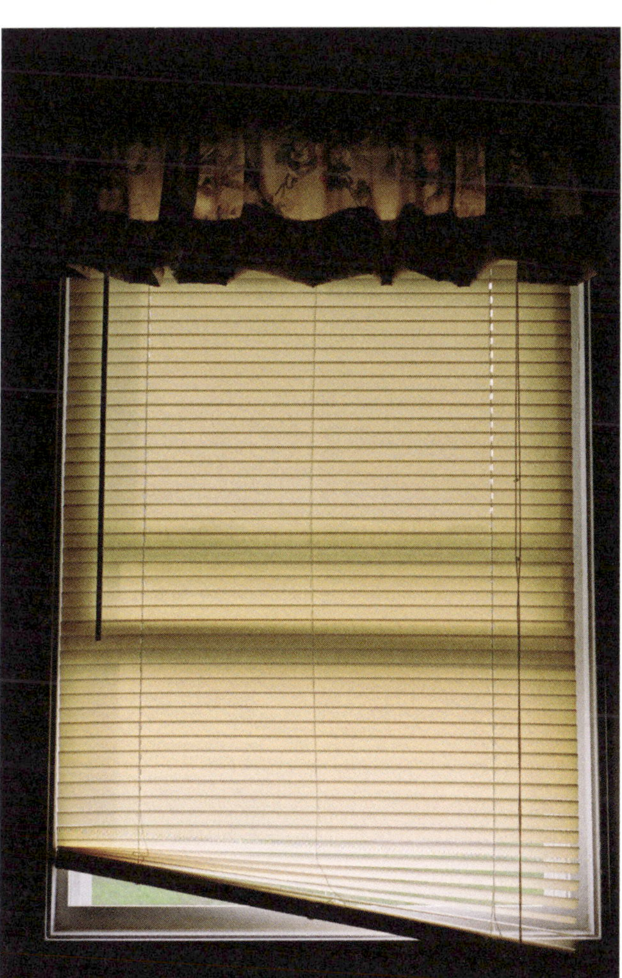

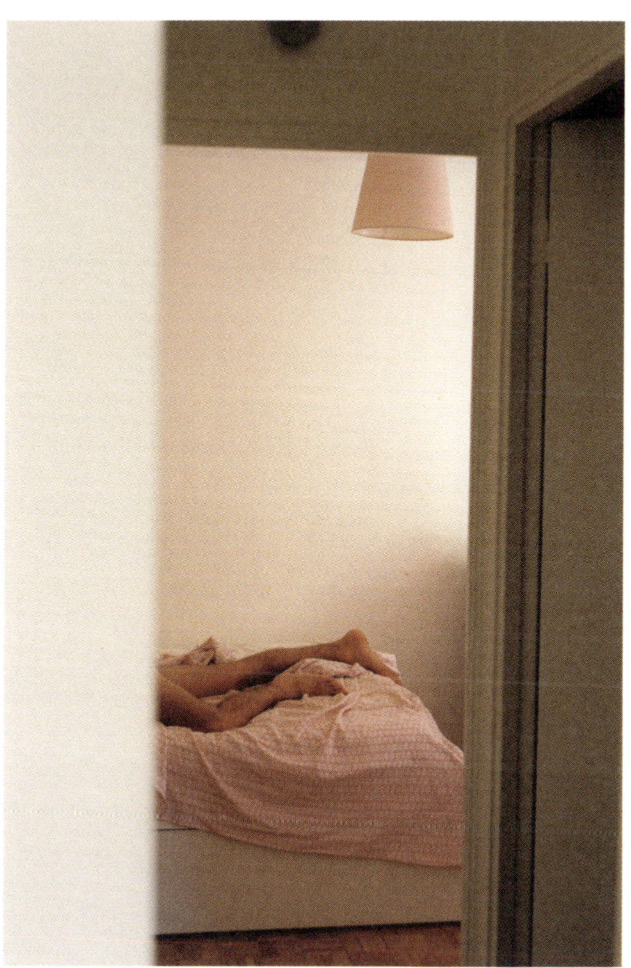

Racoon

Poor me
I am only one thing
PROOL TON CYR
NO TY PRO CLOOR
PROCYON LOTOR
Will I ever be enough

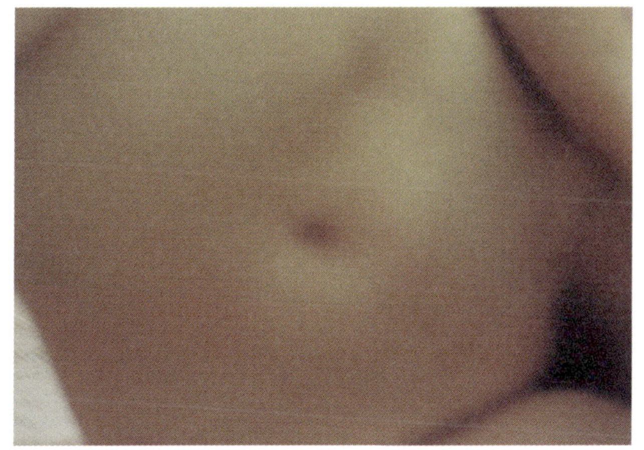

Treasure Island

Treasure Island
You stole my heart
Or maybe it was somebody else's
Who has a heart anyway
I know I have many

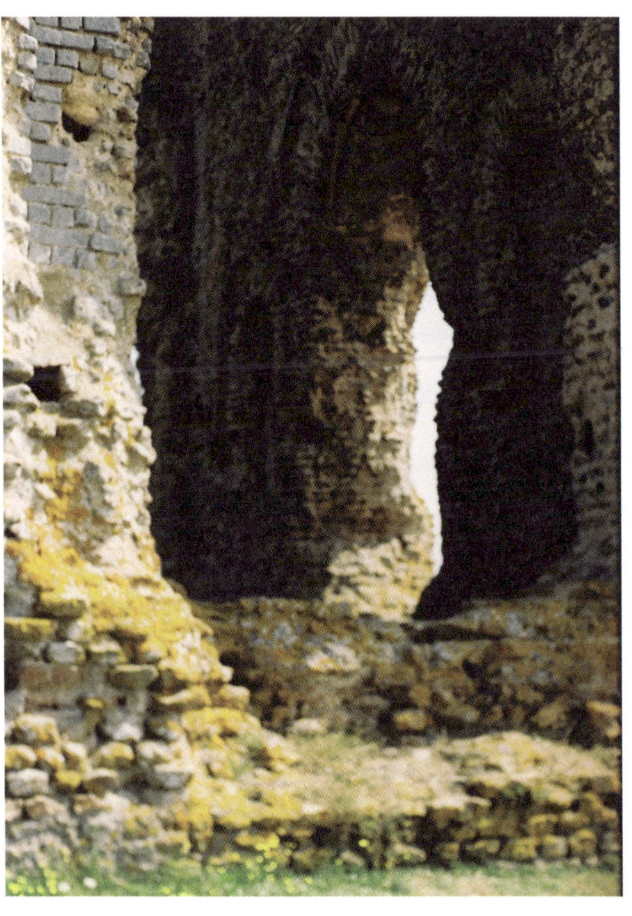

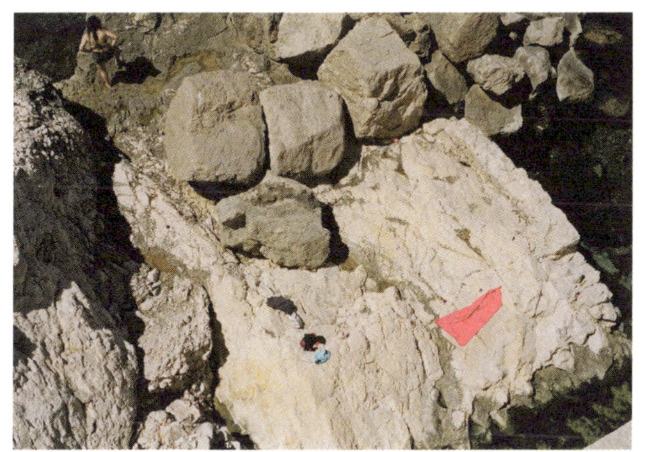

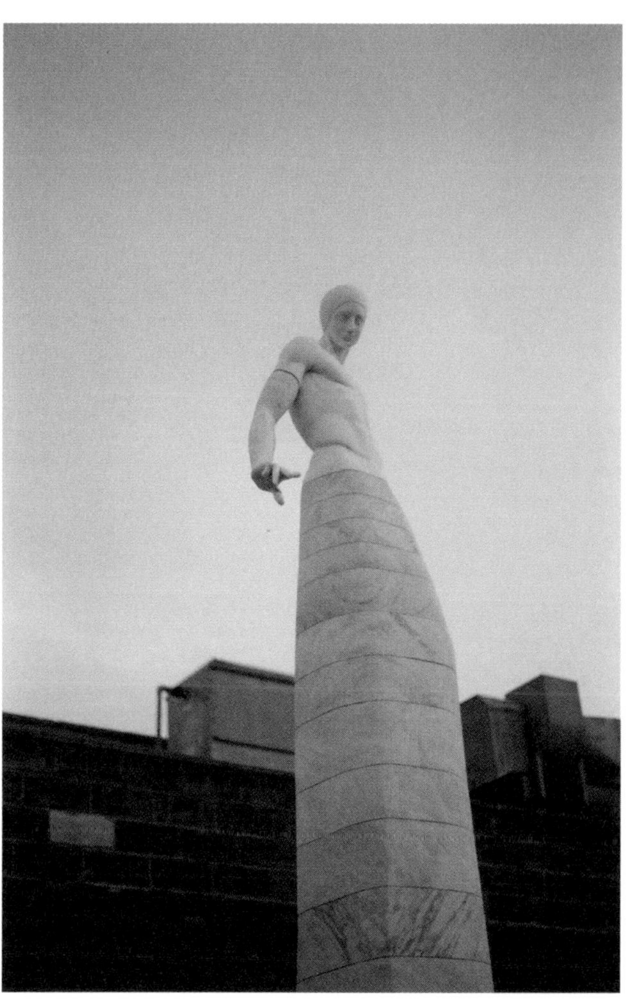

What I Wish He Was Thinking

She was wearing a pair of men's shorts
I hoped they were nobody's
And I tried to imagine her
Buying a pair of men's shorts
For herself
The image was plausible
So I smiled at her
She knew she looked cute in those shorts

I Stay

I will stay here
Still
Lying down or standing still
Can you say lying still
What does standing down mean
I will stay still
Except for the days
I stand strong

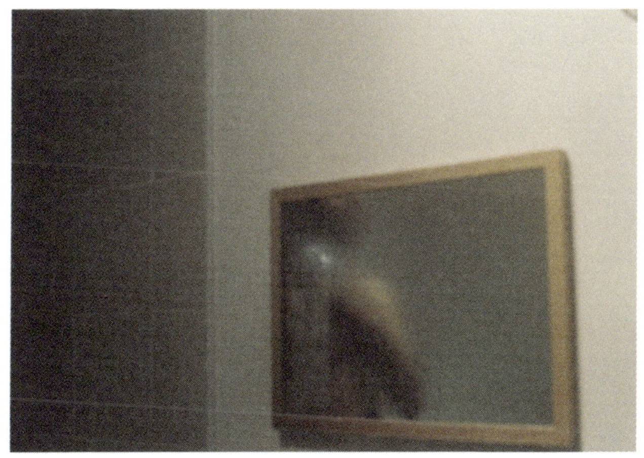

One Fine Day

Your skin is burning
Is the sun too strong
Or could it be the salt
You lick your delicious wounds
Could it be the salt
Making your wounds delicious
Or is it the sun
Covering everything
With gold

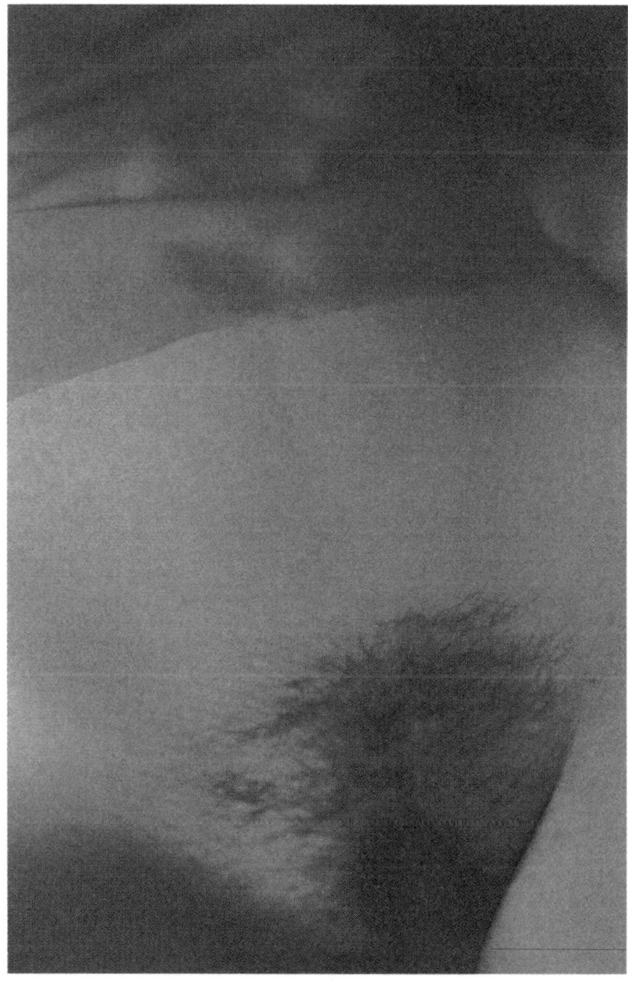

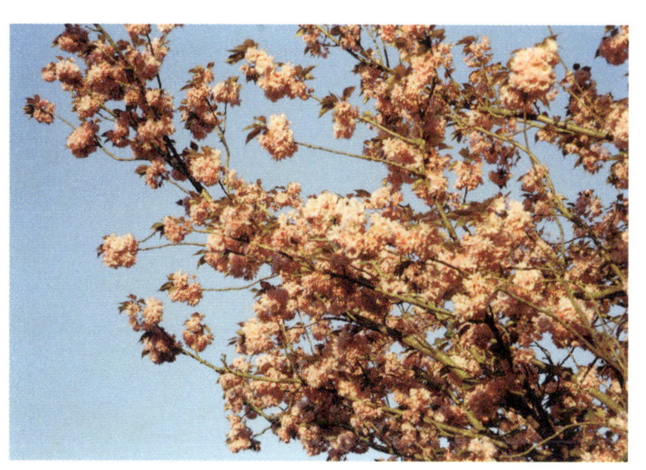

Day Dreaming Peeping Tom

Are you just day dreaming
Your eyes wandering
Your brain wondering how many
We all must be

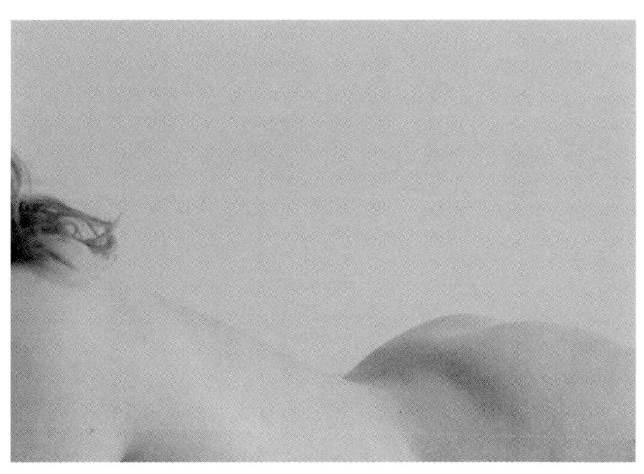

Where Do You Stand

So many questions
Such as
Where do you stand
How tall are you
How are you so tall
And I always wonder
How you can be ok
On an airplane

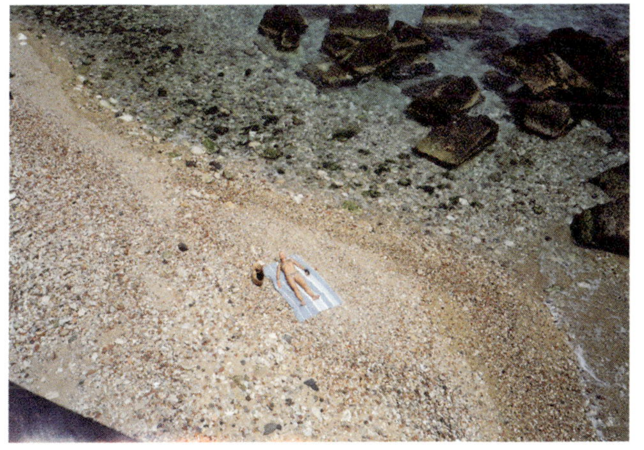

Your Big Body

You pull me up
When I fall down
Which isn't often
Thank god
Or am I just pulling everyone up
All the time
Including you

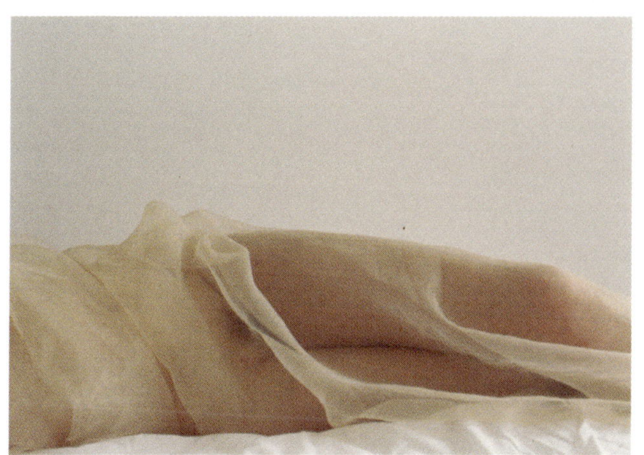

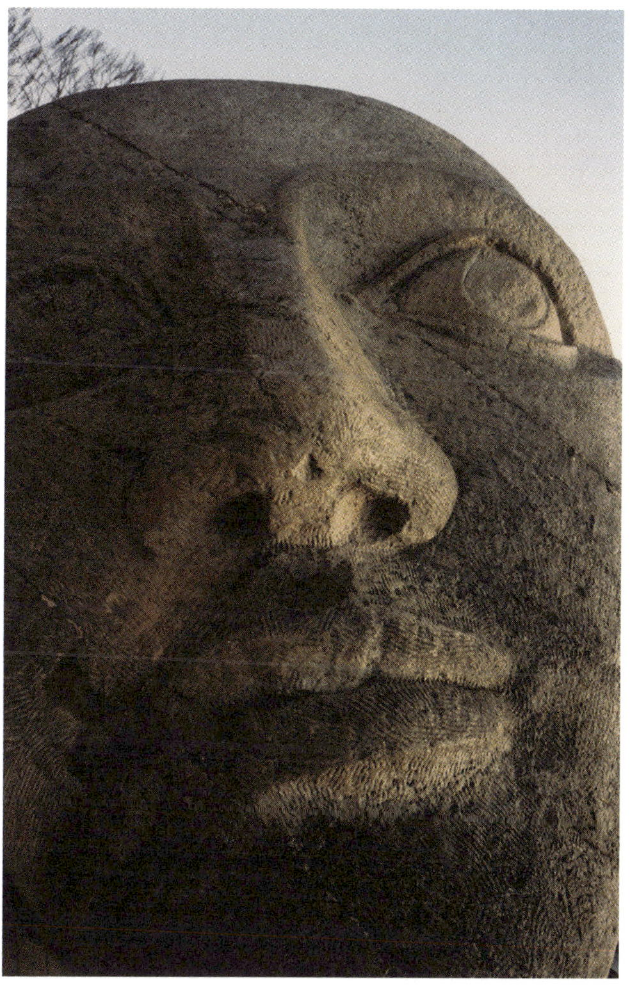

Kink

Have you ever met someone
Who had a foot fetish
I only met a boy who joked about it
And I am still wondering
I think feet are pretty
More than hands
But I like hands better

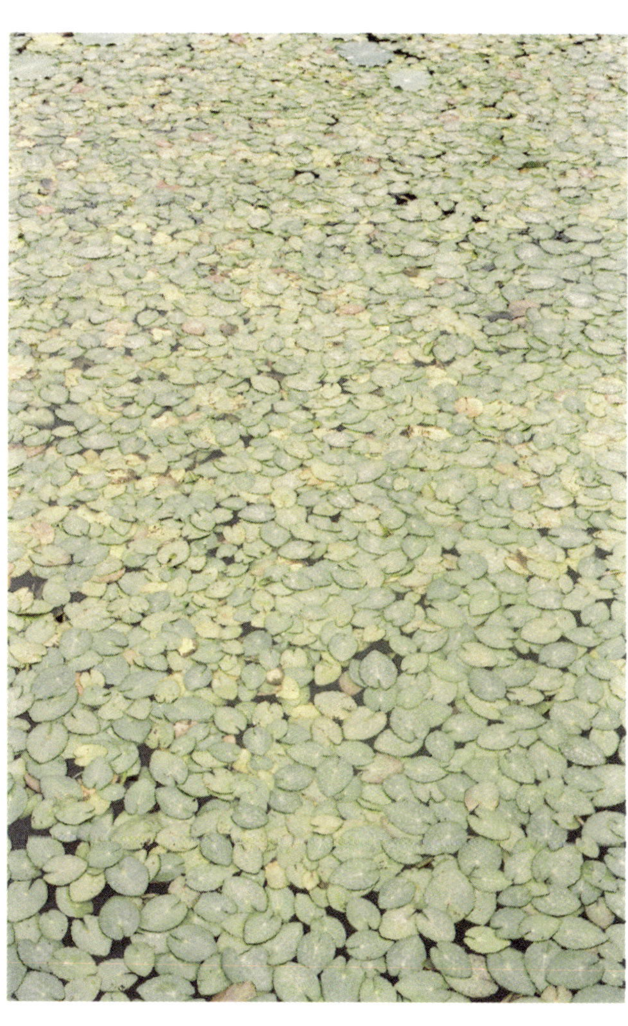

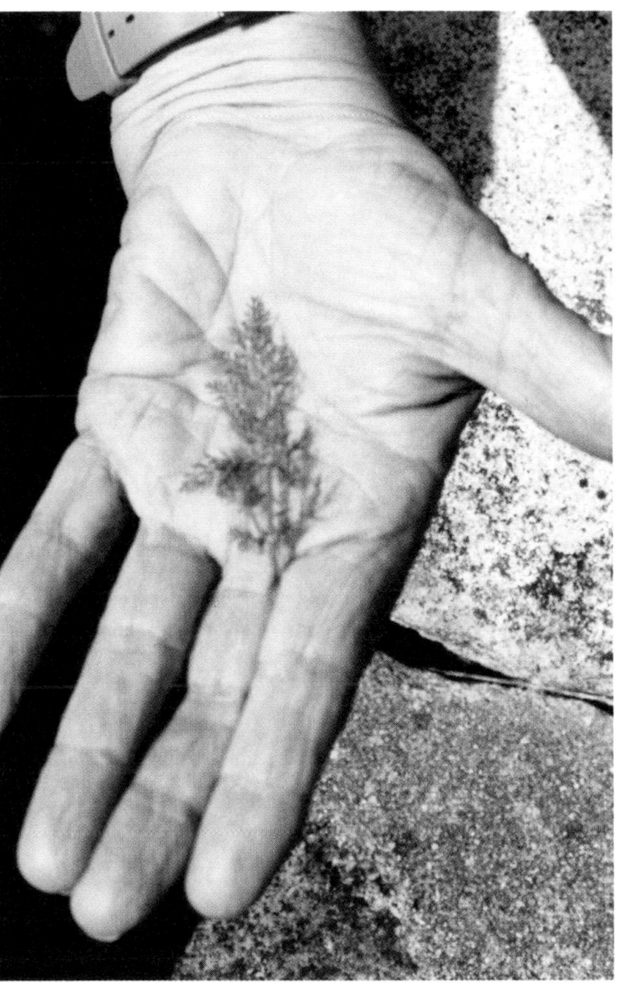

Can I Borrow This Chair

She asked
Can I borrow this chair
And the lady answered
Of course
It's not mine
I was merely keeping it company

Gone

All those things
I kept in my pockets

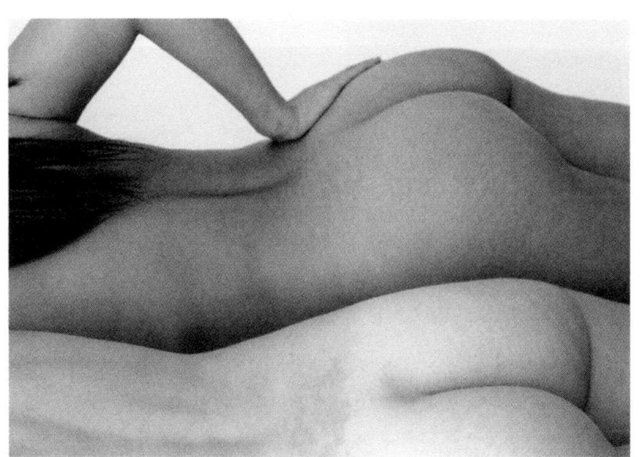

The Sounds Your House Makes

I like when the toaster pops
Cling
That sound is hot
But I don't like
My toast too warm
I don't like
When the butter melts too fast
All breakfast noises
Are nice

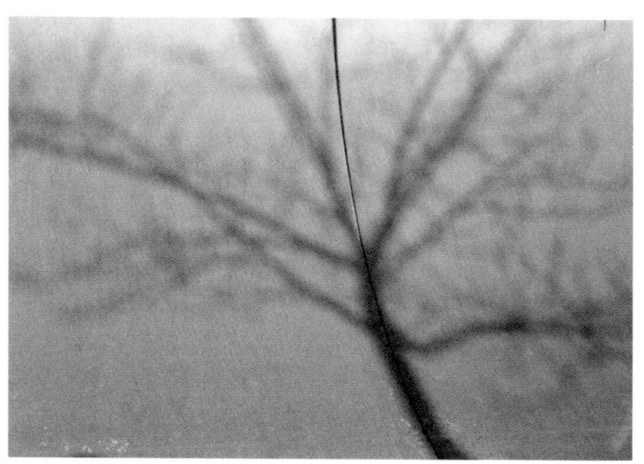

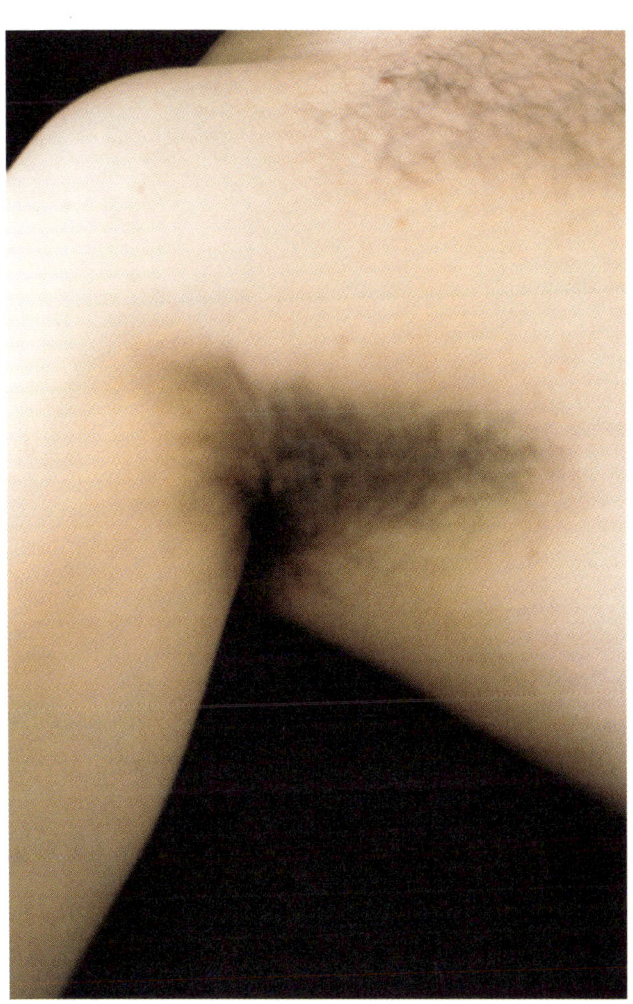

Again

I forgot my glasses
Fuck
It's gonna hurt tomorrow

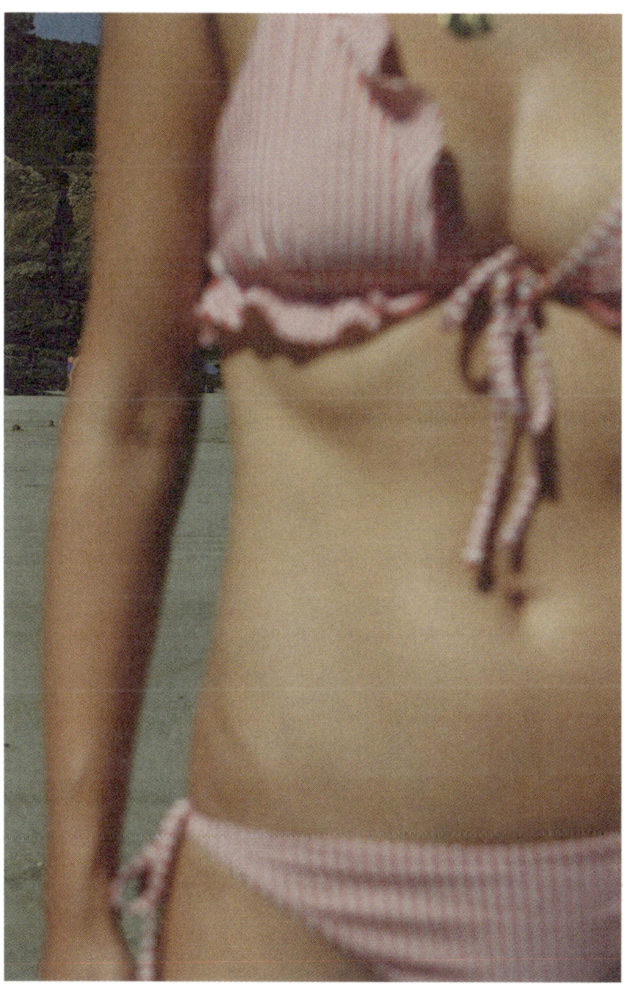

Polistes Bellicosus

It first was a menace
Turning
Buzzing
Around me
Inside the house
Around the car
Hoping I don't get stung
I found myself smiling

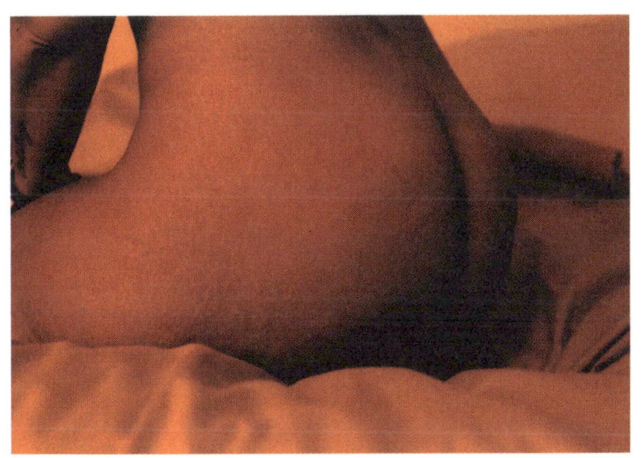

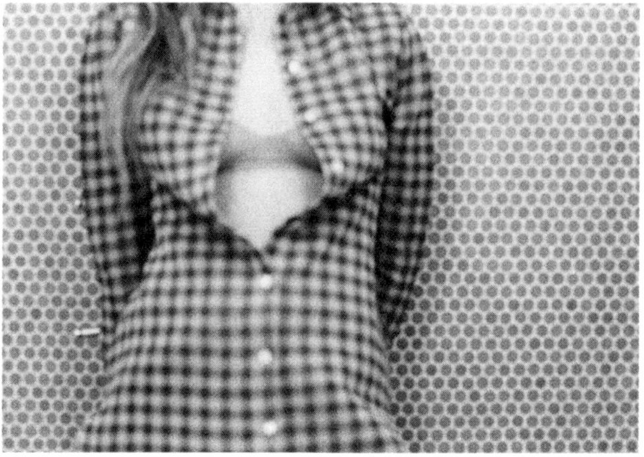

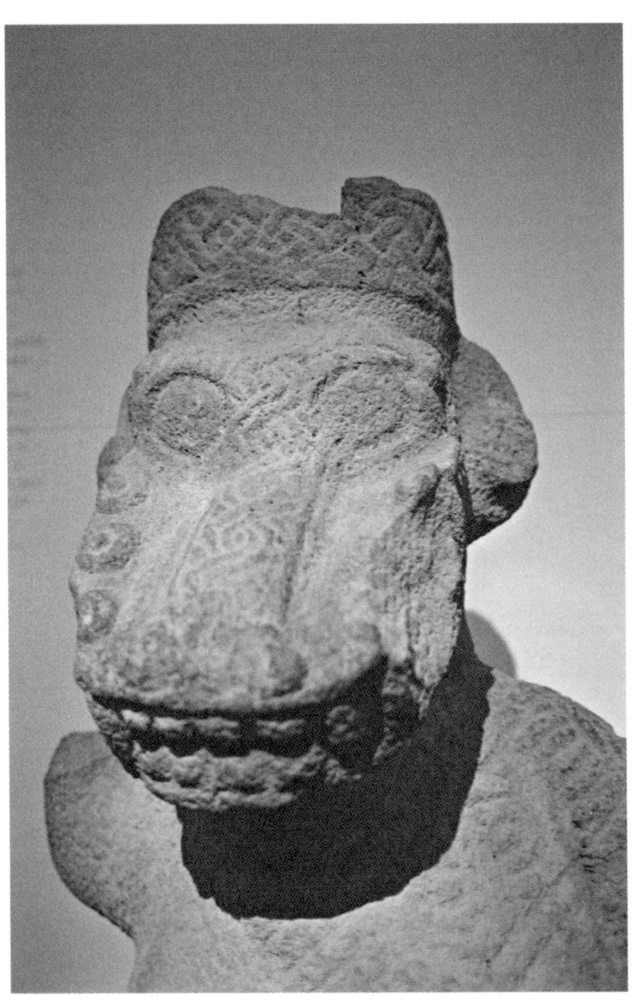

Ha Ha

Do you write
Ha ha
Or
Ah ah
I usually write
Hi hi
But then people read
Hello hello

Getting Around

I squint
To make sure
I don't run over anyone

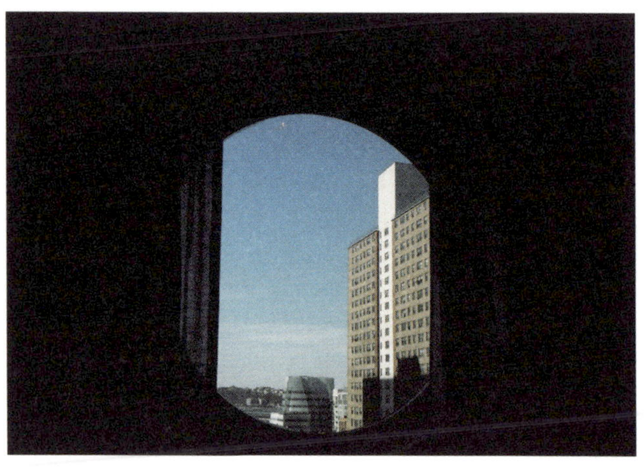

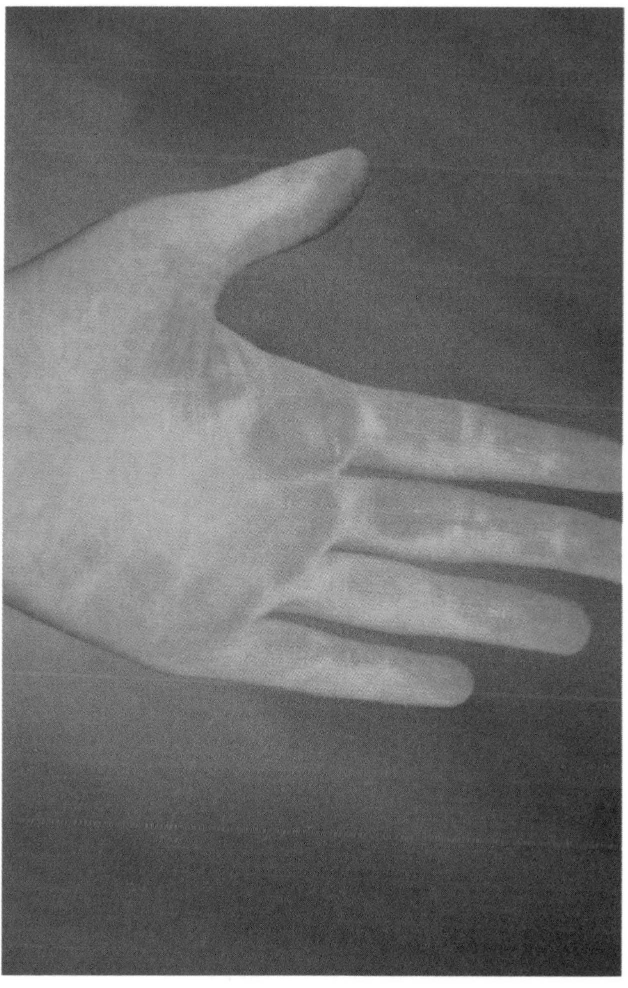

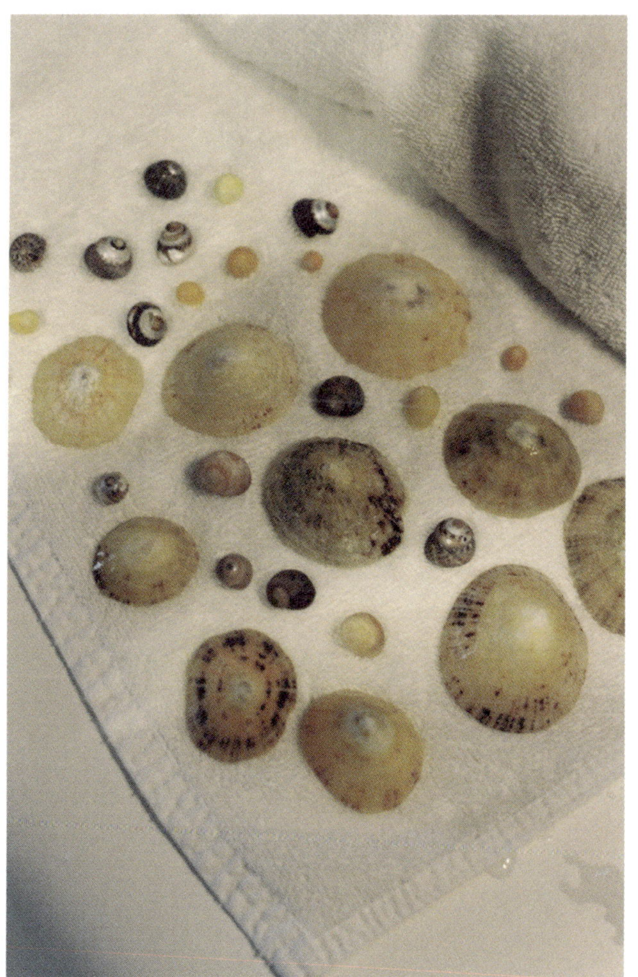

The Myth

It is actually true
If you speak
Extremely
Quietly
On one hand
I can hear you
On the other hand

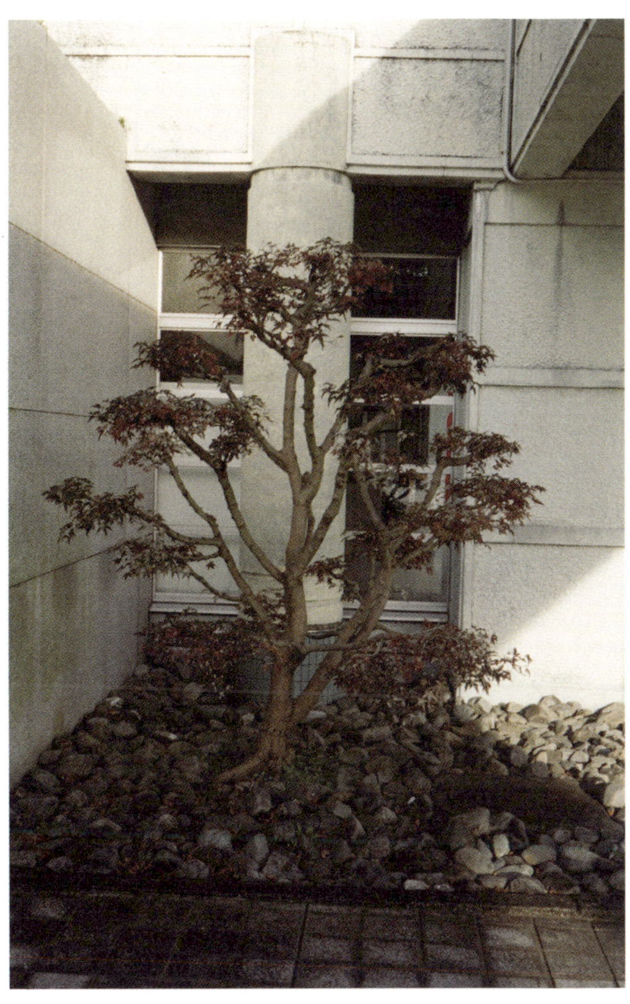

Porn Poem

What is
A porn poem
Is it a poem about porn
It is basically
The same word

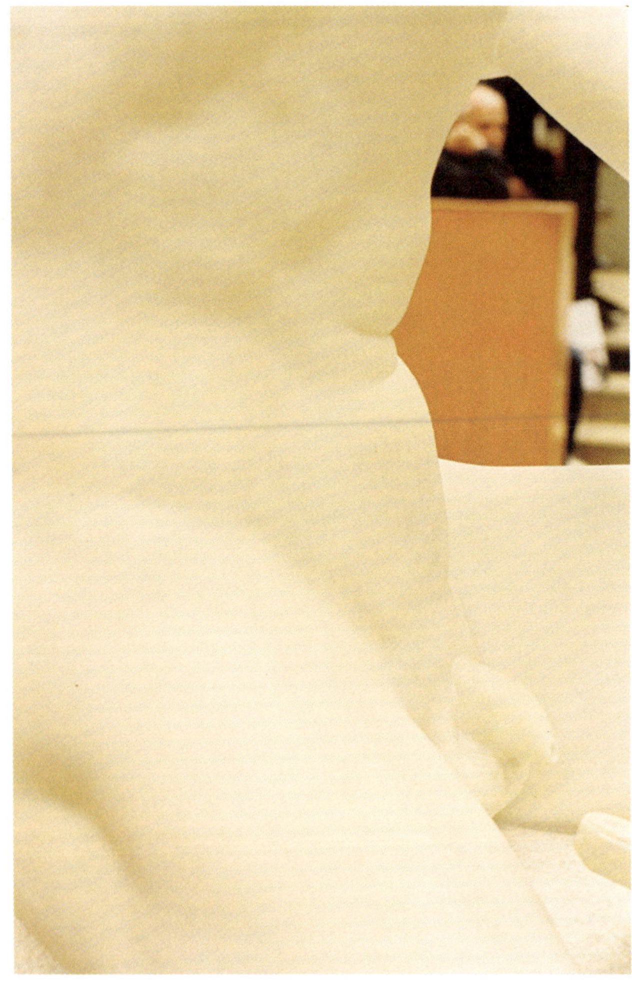

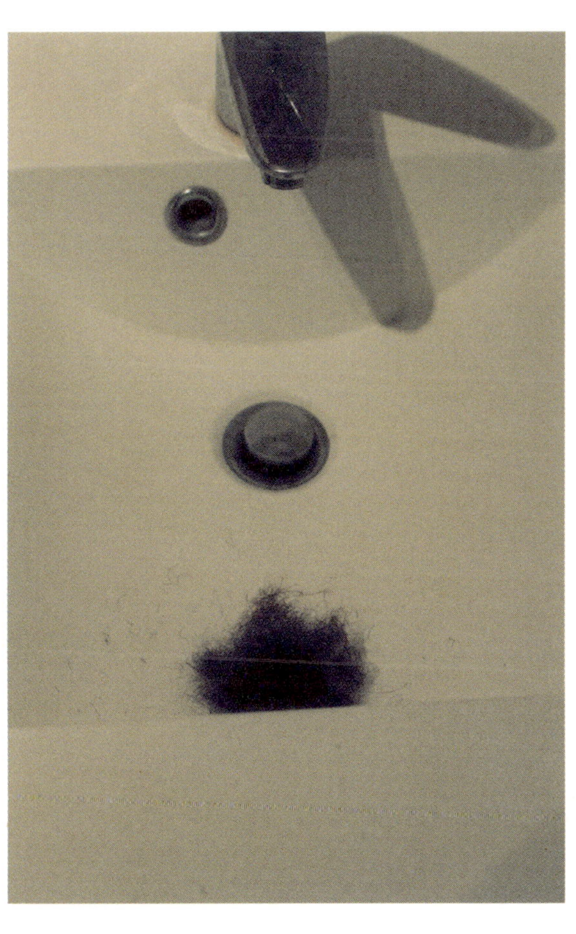

Your Smile

You smile as you lean in
Towards my mouth
I've been meaning to tell you
How sweet your lower lip is
When you were biting mine
We started laughing

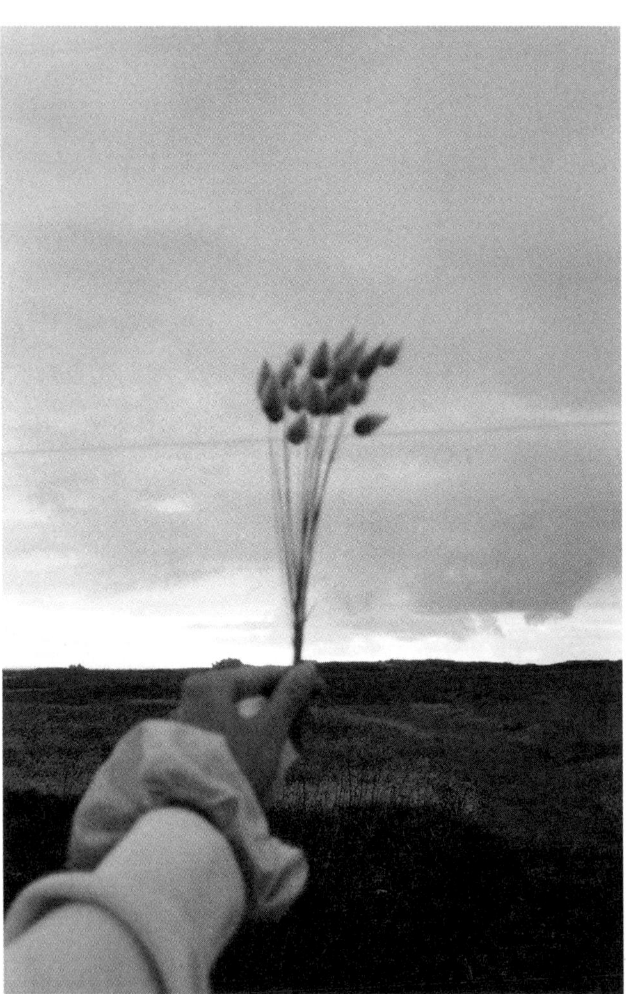

She Sells Seashells By The Seashore

The
Seashore
She
Sells
Seashells
By
By what

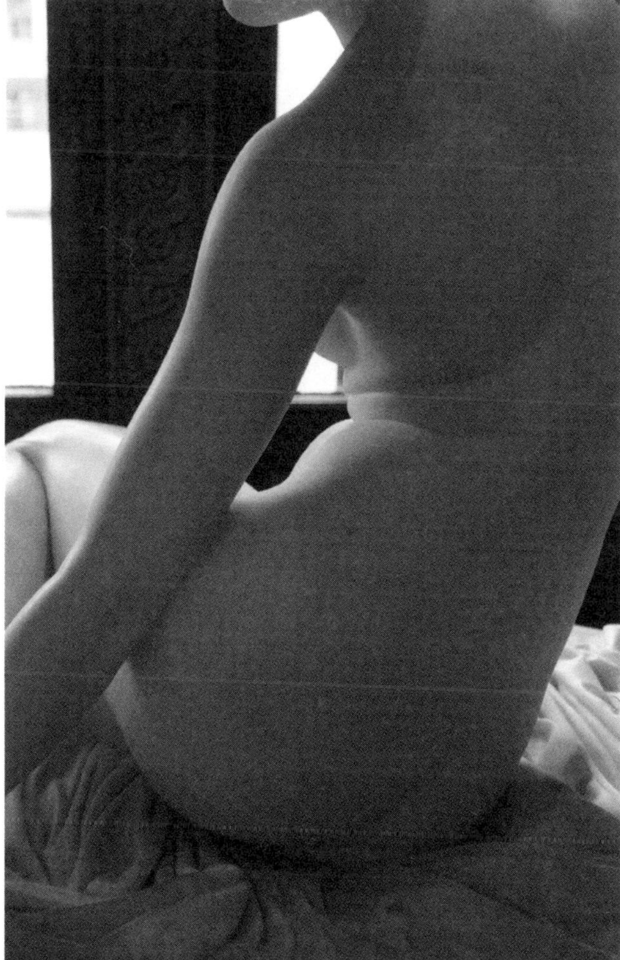

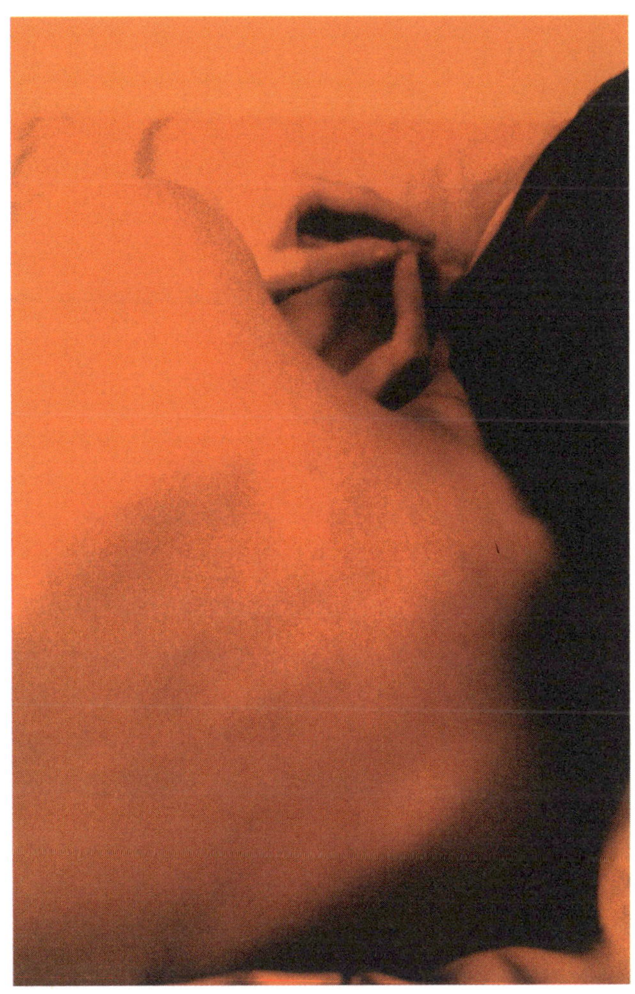

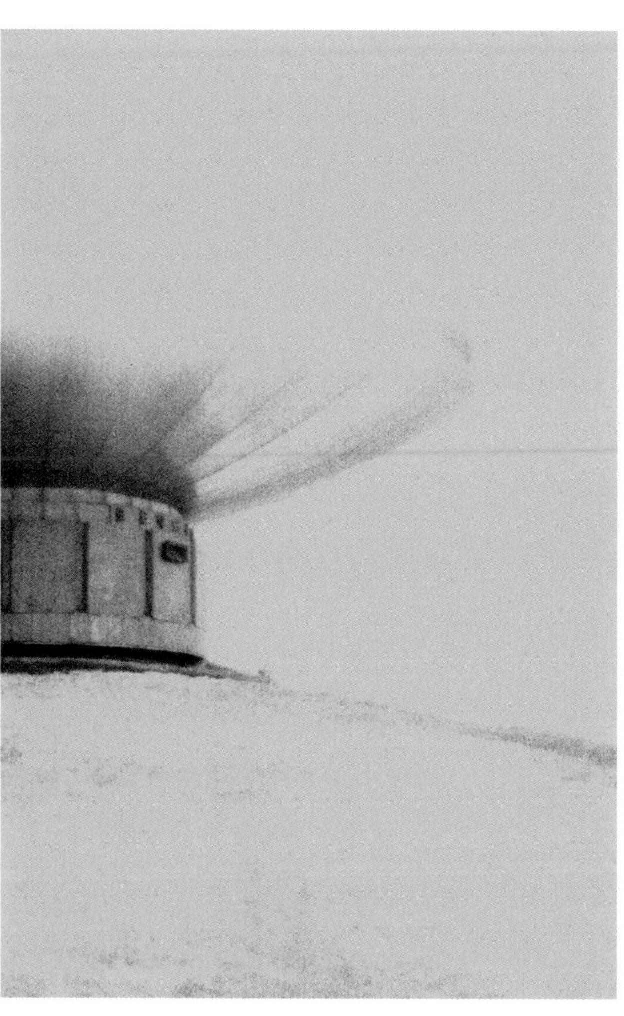

Apollo You Broke My Heart

I entered your temple
After a long hike
And it felt like home
I wept and then
went down for a swim

In The Words Of Harrison Ford

'You have made me laugh
And I'm gonna get the hell
Outta here
Before you make me cry'

APE#160
Marie Déhé & Haydée Touitou
We Have Been Meaning To
© 2020, Art Paper Editions
ISBN 9789493146402
www.artpapereditions.org
www.haydeetouitou.com
www.mariedehe.com

Graphic design:
6'56" (www.6m56s.com)

Edition of 750
Printed in Talinn

Thank you to Paul, Micheline, Alexandra, Donia, Samira, Marina C, Marina D, Léa, Jayme, Jacqueline Feldman for editing the poems, and Camille Vivier for introducing us.